Albert
PUJOLS

by Geoffrey M. Horn

GARETH**STEVENS**
GS
PUBLISHING
A Member of the WRC Media Family of Companies

Please visit our web site at: www.garethstevens.com
For a free color catalog describing Gareth Stevens Publishing's
list of high-quality books and multimedia programs, call
1-800-542-2595 (USA) or 1-800-387-3178 (Canada).
Gareth Stevens Publishing's fax: (414) 332-3567.

Library of Congress Cataloging-in-Publication Data

Horn, Geoffrey M.
    Albert Pujols / by Geoffrey M. Horn.
    p. cm. — (Today's superstars: sports)
    Includes bibliographical references and index.
    ISBN 0-8368-6185-X (lib. bdg.)
    1. Pujols, Albert, 1980—Juvenile literature. 2. Baseball players—
Dominican Republic—Biography—Juvenile literature. I. Title.
GV865.P83H67   2006
796.357092—dc22   2005028960

This edition first published in 2006 by
Gareth Stevens Publishing
A Member of the WRC Media Family of Companies
330 West Olive Street, Suite 100
Milwaukee, WI 53212 USA

This edition copyright © 2006 by Gareth Stevens, Inc.

Editor: Jim Mezzanotte
Art direction and design: Tammy West
Picture research: Diane Laska-Swanke

Photo credits: Cover, © Stephen Green/MLB Photos via Getty Images;
pp. 5, 9, 11, 21, 23, 26, 28 © AP/Wide World Photos; pp. 13, 19 © Scott
Rovak/AFP/Getty Images; p. 17 © Jeff Gross/Getty Images

Printed in the United States of America

1 2 3 4 5 6 7 8 9 10 09 08 07 06

CONTENTS

CHAPTER 1

THE MAN

Stan "The Man" Musial holds a special place in the history of the St. Louis Cardinals baseball team. The Cards' outfielder and first baseman was in twenty-four All-Star Games. He won the National League Most Valuable Player (MVP) award three times. In his career, he had 3,630 hits, 475 home runs, and a batting average of .331. When he retired, he held seventeen major league records. No wonder people still call him "The Man."

There's a new man on the Cardinals these days. The Cards have many fine ballplayers. Right now, they're one of the best clubs in baseball. But there's only one player on the Cards who deserves to

FACT FILE

Albert Pujols stands 6 feet, 3 inches (1.9 meters) tall. He weighs 225 pounds (102 kilograms). His full name is José Alberto Pujols. The last name is pronounced POO-holes.

be called The Man. His name is Albert Pujols. Stan Musial calls Pujols the best right-handed hitter in the game today.

Big Numbers

Pujols joined the Cards in 2001. Since then, he has already put up Hall of Fame numbers. In August 2005, he became the first player to hit thirty homers in each of his first five major league seasons.

Later that same month, he knocked in his hundredth run for the year. Pujols is the fourth player in major league history to get 100 runs batted in (RBIs) in his first five seasons. The other three are Ted Williams, Joe DiMaggio, and Al Simmons. All three rank among the greatest hitters who ever lived. Like Musial, they are all in the National Baseball Hall of Fame.

In his first five seasons with the Cardinals, Pujols established himself as one of the best hitters in baseball history.

5

Stunning as his numbers are, Pujols would rather not talk about them. "I want to win," he says. "The numbers are going to be there if you help your team win. If you play the game the right way. Move a guy over. Steal a base. Make some plays. That's when your numbers are going to be there."

Hard Work, Quick Hands

The Cards' first baseman has worked hard to get where he is today. He works out with weights to make his forearms stronger. He spends hours in the batting cage improving his swing. When he's not on the field, he studies videos of his swing. By doing so, he can avoid falling into bad habits when he bats.

A former teammate, Tino Martinez, praises the Pujols work ethic. "Every single day of the season he has a routine,

FACT FILE

Joe DiMaggio played center field for the New York Yankees from 1936 to 1951. He set a record in 1941 by getting at least one hit in fifty-six straight games. Pujols has one of the longest hitting streaks in recent years. He hit in thirty games straight in 2003.

Measuring Success

In baseball, there are many ways to measure hitting. Each day, newspapers publish lists of league leaders in batting. Pujols is often listed among the leaders in batting average, runs scored, RBIs, hits, and home runs.

At the end of his fifth season, Pujols had a career batting average of .332. What does this number mean? To find a player's batting average, you divide the number of hits by the number of at bats. A player who has 300 hits in 1,000 at bats has a batting average of exactly .300.

The term "at bat" has a special meaning. To find the number of at bats, you start with the number of times a player comes up to hit. You then subtract the number of times the player gets a walk, is hit by the pitch, or hits a sacrifice. A player who comes up to bat 500 times, walks 80 times, makes 15 sacrifice hits, and is hit by the pitch 5 times would have 400 at bats.

Power hitters are often rated by total bases and slugging average. To find a player's total bases, you score one point for each base a player reaches on a safe hit. Getting to first is a single. Getting to second is a double. A triple is reaching third base. A home run counts as four. Suppose a player hits 100 singles, 50 doubles, 10 triples, and 40 home runs. The total number of hits would be 200, or the sum of $100 + 50 + 10 + 40$. The total bases would be 390, or the sum of $100 + (50 \times 2) + (10 \times 3) + (40 \times 4)$.

To find the slugging average, you divide the number of at bats by the number of total bases. At this point in his career, Pujols has a slugging average of better than .620.

and he does his whole routine," says Martinez. "It's unbelievable. There's not a pitch he can't hit. There are no holes in his swing. He has a game plan for every pitcher. He knows what he wants to do."

When Pujols comes to the plate, he stands at the back of the batter's box. He raises his bat high, and he puts much of his weight on the back foot. He keeps his hands back, waiting as long as possible to commit himself.

The key to hitting is the hands, he says. "Even if you jump at the ball, your hands are back," he told an interviewer. "What's most important is for my hands to be in the right position for me to drive the ball. If it's away, I can drive the ball away. If it's inside, I can pull the ball down the line."

FACT FILE

Pujols isn't fast, but he's improving as a base runner. In his first four seasons, he stole a total of 13 bases. He was caught stealing 13 times. Figures for 2005 tell a different story. By the end of the season, he had stolen 16 bases and had been thrown out only twice.

In the 2005 playoffs, Pujols hit a dramatic three-run homer in the ninth inning against relief pitcher Brad Lidge of the Houston Astros. The Cards won the game, 5-4, but Houston went on to win the National League Championship series.

BASEBALL FEVER

José Alberto Pujols was born
January 16, 1980. He grew
up in Santo Domingo,
the capital of the
Dominican Republic. His father,
Bienvenido Pujols, was a pitcher
in the Dominican league.

Love for the Game

Few families had enough money to buy
baseball gloves and bats for their children.
As a young boy, Alberto played baseball
with whatever he could find. He made
a "glove" out of a cardboard carton. He
used a big stick for a bat. Alberto and
his friends played catch with limes.

"I lived to play baseball," Pujols says.
As long as he could play ball, he was
happy. He also watched U.S. teams on
TV. Whenever possible, he went to the
ballpark to see his father pitch.

In Alberto's big family, there were a
dozen children. The other kids belonged

¡Viva Béisbol!

Baseball — or *béisbol* in Spanish — is more than just a sport in the Dominican Republic. It's a passion. Dominicans have been playing baseball for more than a hundred years. Even the smallest, poorest towns have ballparks. The country has its own pro league. Its pro season begins in October and ends in February.

More than four hundred Dominicans have played in the major leagues in the United States. Like Pujols, batting stars Vladimir Guerrero and Miguel Tejada come from this small Caribbean nation. So do Manny Ramirez, David Ortiz, and pitcher Pedro Martinez. Scouts for U.S. teams travel all over the Dominican looking for good young ballplayers.

Twelve- and thirteen-year-olds compete at a baseball camp in the Dominican Republic. Scouts for U.S. teams often show up at games like this one, looking for hot young talent.

to his father's brothers and sisters. He
was the youngest child. Heading the
household was Alberto's grandmother.
She was a woman of deep faith. She
raised her grandson to share her values.

The Road to Independence
During the 1990s, more than 250,000
people left the Dominican Republic for
the United States. They wanted better
jobs at better pay. They also wanted to
make a better life for themselves and their
children. Some members of the Pujols
family moved to New York City. In 1996,
his father made the move, too. Alberto,
who was sixteen, went with him.

The Pujols family didn't stay in New
York very long. Costs were too high,
and there was too much crime. They
didn't feel safe in the nation's largest city.
So, they moved to the Midwest. The town

FACT FILE

The Dominican Republic is part of the island of Hispaniola. This
island lies southeast of the United States. When Pujols was born,
the country had about 5.6 million people. Today, about 9 million
people live there.

A Man Among Boys

David Fry was the baseball coach when Pujols was in high school. "Albert was a man among the boys," Fry later told a local reporter. Pujols was muscular and more than 6 feet (1.8 m) tall. He was so big and so strong that some parents thought he must be older than sixteen.

Fry still remembers a home run that Pujols hit as a teenager. The ball rocketed over the left field fence. It traveled at least 450 feet (137 m) before slamming into an air-conditioning unit on top of a two-story building.

Pujols wowed fans at the Cardinals' 2001 home opener by hitting a home run off starting pitcher Denny Neagle of the Colorado Rockies.

they chose was Independence, Missouri. Independence is near Kansas City. It has a population of about 112,000, including a small Dominican community.

Pujols enrolled at Fort Osage High School. He had a tough time at first, because his English was poor. He tried hard to fit in. He worked on his language skills, and he shortened his name from Alberto to Albert.

In baseball, he let his bat do most of the talking. Playing shortstop, he led his high school team to the state championship in 1997. His former teammates are thrilled by his success in the pros. But they still tease him about his high school days. "I hope he has a better car," pitcher Chris Francka told a local newspaper. "We wouldn't let him drive to any games in that thing he had because we didn't think he would make it."

FACT FILE

"I try to spend as much time as possible with God and my family," Pujols says today. "That's more important than anything I am doing in baseball."

UPS AND DOWNS

One night in 1998, Pujols went to a Latin dance club in Kansas City. He was eighteen years old. People in the club were supposed to be at least twenty-one. Albert looked older than his age, and he was able to get inside.

At the club, he met an attractive young woman. Her name was Deidre, but her friends called her Dee-Dee. She spoke little Spanish. Albert's English wasn't great. But he spoke well enough to get her phone number and ask for a date.

Albert and Dee-Dee
On their first date, Albert said he had a confession to make. He had lied about his age at the club. Dee-Dee immediately felt she could trust him. She told him the truth about herself. She had recently

given birth to a baby daughter. The girl, named Isabella, had a birth defect. Baby Bella had Down syndrome.

Albert was still in high school. Dee-Dee wasn't sure if he was ready to deal with a special-needs child. But she gave him pamphlets written in Spanish about Down syndrome. When Albert met Bella, he said he wanted to help raise the child as his own.

Albert and Dee-Dee were married on January 1, 2000. She jokes that she chose New Year's Day for a reason. She wanted to make it easy for Albert to remember their anniversary.

Scouting Reports

Pujols finished high school in 1998. To be near Dee-Dee and Bella, he enrolled at a community college in the Kansas City area. In his first game for the college's team, he hit a grand slam home run.

FACT FILE

Albert and Deidre Pujols added a second child to their family in 2001. In January of that year, Deidre gave birth to a boy. His name is Alberto, Jr., or A.J.

What is Down Syndrome?

Our bodies have billions of tiny cells. In a baby born with Down syndrome, these cells grow in a way that is different from that of other babies. Each year, about four thousand babies in the United States are born with Down syndrome.

Children with Down syndrome develop more slowly than others. Most will learn how to walk, talk, get dressed, and take care of themselves. But they often learn these skills much later than other children. Some Down syndrome children also have physical problems. They may have trouble seeing, hearing, or breathing normally. Heart problems are common.

All children need love and support from teachers, family, and friends. Children with Down syndrome need extra help to develop their skills and talents. Because of their experience with Bella, Albert and Deidre have tried to help other kids with special needs.

Deidre and Albert Pujols celebrate his team's victory over the Los Angeles Dodgers in the first round of the 2004 playoffs.

Pro scouts began watching Pujols play. They admired his high batting average and long home runs. They were less impressed with his defense. They didn't think shortstop was the right place for him. They also thought he was too slow. His lack of foot speed didn't matter when he smashed the ball high and far over the outfield fence. But it was a big problem when he tried to run out an infield hit or stretch a single into a double.

The Cardinals were willing to sign him. They just didn't want to pay him much money. Pujols was discouraged. He wasn't sure he was good enough to make the major leagues. But Dee-Dee and her family helped raise his spirits. "I prayed about it," Albert says. "God blessed me and gave me the chance." When the Cards upped their offer to $65,000, he grabbed it.

FACT FILE

The Tampa Bay Devil Rays flew Pujols down to Florida in 1999. They tried him out as a catcher, but he didn't like that position. The Rays decided to pass on Pujols. "That was obviously the biggest mistake we made when I was in Tampa Bay," the team's top scout said later.

The Baseball Draft

Most young players are not free to pick the major league team of their choice. Instead, teams get together each year to choose, or "draft," the top young prospects. In the draft, the teams take turns choosing the players they want to sign. The hottest prospects are picked in the early rounds. Others are chosen later. The teams rely on reports from scouts in making their decisions.

The Cards waited until the thirteenth round to pick Pujols in 1999. About four hundred players were chosen before him. In 2005, the Cards chose Albert's cousin, Wilfrido Pujols, in the sixth round. He was the two hundredth pick overall. The Cards signed Wilfrido to a contract for $120,000.

Albert has worked hard to improve his base running. Here, he beats a tag by catcher Damian Miller of the Arizona Diamondbacks.

MAKING THE MAJORS

"I knew if I was good enough, I would make it to the big leagues in three or four years." That's what Albert Pujols thought when he signed with the Cardinals in 1999. But he was wrong. Pujols needed only a year in the minor leagues to win a starting job in St. Louis.

Playing in Peoria
In 2000, his first season of pro ball, the Cards sent Pujols to Peoria, Illinois. He played third base for the Peoria Chiefs, in the Class A Midwest League. The Chiefs

FACT FILE
The Cardinals named Pujols their Minor League Player of the Year in 2000.

ranked low in the Cards' farm system of minor league teams. Like other teams in the majors, the Cards used this system to develop new players. Albert only earned $252 every two weeks. "We were truly living on love," recalls Deidre. "We ate a lot of mac 'n' cheese in those days."

The Chiefs' manager, Tom Lawless, remembers Pujols as a very good student. "He worked hard and wanted to learn," says Lawless. "He had the same problems a lot of young players have when he got frustrated and he didn't run out some ground balls. We had a little chat and took care of that. I told him, 'Don't make yourself look bad.' He was a good kid."

In a 2005 game against the San Diego Padres, Pujols snagged a line drive at first base to start a rare triple play.

Albert tore up the league. He finished first in slugging average (.565) and second in batting average (.324). He was voted the league MVP. Late in the season, the Cards moved him up to the Triple-A Memphis Redbirds, one of their top farm clubs. He batted .367 in seven playoff games, and his 13th-inning home run made the Redbirds league champions.

Rookie of the Year

Pujols did so well as a minor league player that the Cards decided to bring him to spring training in 2001. He was not expected to make the club. But he had a sizzling spring. He led the team in total bases (34) and batting average (.349).

He got a big break when Cards player Bobby Bonilla was injured, leaving a spot open on the team's roster. Pujols was a surprise starter in left field on opening

FACT FILE

The Cards' first baseman Mark McGwire retired at the end of the 2001 season. During his career, he hit 583 home runs. Pujols became the Cards' full-time first baseman in 2004.

Home Runs and Strikeouts

Many home run hitters take a huge swing. When they make contact, they hit the ball a long way, but they also strike out a lot. Reggie Jackson is a good example. In twenty-one major league seasons, he hit 563 home runs. But he struck out 2,597 times — almost five strikeouts for every home run.

Albert Pujols is different. He's a line-drive hitter who can also hit for power. For a player who has already set home run records, his strikeout total is very low. During his rookie season, he hit 37 homers and struck out 93 times. By 2004, he was even better. In 154 games that year, he hit 46 homers and struck out only 52 times!

Albert shows his sweet stroke as he blasts a grand slam homer against the Cincinnati Reds.

day, and he quickly became a fan favorite. On April 9, he became the first Cards rookie in forty-seven years to hit a home run in the club's home opener.

During his amazing rookie season, Pujols started almost every game. He usually played third base or outfield, but he also filled in at first base for the aging slugger Mark McGwire. Albert led the team in batting average (.329), hits (194), home runs (37), doubles (47), RBIs (130), and runs scored (112). Baseball writers made him their unanimous pick as National League Rookie of the Year.

The only down note was the Cards' weak performance in the playoffs. In a best-of-five series against the Arizona Diamondbacks, Pujols got only 2 hits (including a home run) in 18 at bats. Arizona went on to win the World Series.

FACT FILE

Pujols finished fourth in the voting for National League MVP in 2001. In the American League, Ichiro Suzuki won both Rookie of the Year and MVP honors.

HUNDRED MILLION DOLLAR MAN

After a fantastic rookie season, Pujols continued to post eye-popping numbers. In 2002, he again led his team in batting (.314), home runs (34), RBIs (127), and runs scored (118). He did even better in 2003. His thirty-game hitting streak was tops in the majors, and his .359 batting average ranked first in the National League. Pujols had 212 hits in 2003, including 51 doubles and 43 homers. He drove in 124 runs and scored 137. *The Sporting News* named him Player of the Year.

FACT FILE

Pujols isn't the highest paid player in baseball. Alex Rodriguez, or "A-Rod," has a ten-year, $252 million deal. Second to him is Derek Jeter, with $189 million for ten years. A-Rod and Jeter play for the New York Yankees.

Playoff MVP

How good is Albert Pujols? Just ask the Houston Astros. They got a lot more Pujols than they could handle in October 2004.

Pujols was the series MVP as the Cards beat the Astros for the National League title. In Game 1, he went 2-for-3, with a first-inning home run. He hit another homer to put the Cardinals ahead in Game 2. In the sixth inning of that game, he also made a terrific fielding play. With nobody out and Houston players on first and second, he caught a bunt bare-handed in front of home plate. He threw a bullet to third to beat the lead runner.

Albert went 3-for-4 with 3 RBIs and a home run in Game 4. He had three more hits in Game 6, including his fourth home run of the series. In Game 7, he drove in the tying run with a double down the left-field line. Then he scored the winning run on a homer by Scott Rolen. In the best-of-seven series, he batted 14-for-28, for an average of .500. He led the team with 9 RBIs.

His bat was much quieter in the 2004 World Series against the Red Sox. The Sox swept the Cards in four games. Pujols went 5-for-15, with 2 doubles. But he had no home runs and no RBIs.

Cardinals general manager Walt Jocketty joined Albert in February 2004 to announce the slugger's new seven-year contract. The $100 million deal was the most money the team had ever offered any player.

His fellow players voted him the Major
League Player of the Year.

"Money I Borrowed from God"

Pujols was the biggest bargain in baseball
in 2003. His pay for the whole year was
$950,000. For most people, this amount of
money is huge. But there are part-timers
in the major leagues who earn a lot more.

The St. Louis superstar finally got a
salary equal to his talents in 2004. On
February 20, the Cards announced that
they had signed Pujols to a seven-year,
$100 million contract.

"There's no breaks here," Albert said.
"This is business. You try to get what
you deserve. And that's what I want."
He went on to say that while $100 million
was a lot of money, it really wasn't his.
"It's money I borrowed from God, and He
lets me use it."

FACT FILE

In 2005, Albert and Deidre started the Pujols Family
Foundation. The charity has given money to help children
with Down syndrome in the St. Louis area. It has also sent
money to help kids in the Dominican Republic.

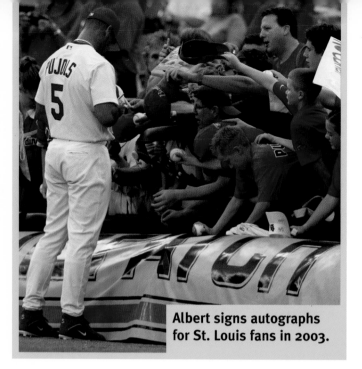

Albert signs autographs for St. Louis fans in 2003.

MVP Season in 2005

The fat contract didn't change his playing style. In 2004, he led the league in total bases (389) and runs scored (133). He crashed 46 homers, knocked in 123 runs, and had a batting average of .331. Pujols had another great year in 2005. He hit .330, with 41 homers and 117 RBIs. Playing just one position — first base — for two whole years also helped his fielding.

Pujols came close to winning regular-season MVP honors in each of his first four years. Finally, in 2005, he captured his first regular-season MVP trophy. He was disappointed the Cards didn't make it to the World Series that year. But with a fine team behind him, and years of playing time ahead of him, he hopes to wear a World Series ring before too long.

TIME LINE

1980 José Alberto Pujols is born January 16 in Santo Domingo, Dominican Republic.

1996 Moves with his father to the United States. After a short time in New York City, they settle in Independence, Missouri.

1997 His high school baseball team wins the state championship.

1999 Picked in the thirteenth round of the major league draft, he signs with the St. Louis Cardinals.

2000 Deidre and Albert Pujols marry on New Year's Day. He has an MVP season as a minor league player.

2001 In his first major league season with the Cardinals, Pujols is voted National League Rookie of the Year.

2002 Places second to Barry Bonds in National League MVP voting. (He also finishes second to Bonds in 2003.)

2004 Pujols is voted MVP in the playoff series against the Houston Astros.

2005 Albert and Deidre set up the Pujols Family Foundation. He hits at least thirty home runs for a fifth straight season. He wins his first National League regular-season MVP trophy.

GLOSSARY

at bats — the number of times a player comes up to hit, minus the number of times the player gets a walk, is hit by the pitch, or hits a sacrifice bunt or sacrifice fly.

batting average — the number of hits divided by the number of at bats.

contract — a legal agreement. In baseball, a player's contract establishes how much a team will pay the player, and for how long.

Down syndrome — a birth defect that can cause children to develop more slowly.

draft — in baseball, a system in which major league teams take turns choosing the young players they want to sign to a contract.

farm clubs — minor league teams that develop players for a team in the major leagues.

runs batted in (RBIs) — runs that score as a direct result of a batter's performance.

sacrifice — in baseball, a bunt or fly ball that allows a teammate to reach another base. A fly ball caught by an outfielder is called a sacrifice fly if a runner scores after the catch.

slugging average — total bases divided by the number of at bats.

TO FIND OUT MORE

BOOKS

The Everything Kids' Baseball Book. Rich Mintzer (Adams Media)

Little League's Official How-To-Play Baseball Book. Peter Kreutzer and Ted Kerley (Broadway Books)

Stan Musial. Baseball Legends (series). John Grabowski (Chelsea House)

VIDEOS

World Series 04: Boston Red Sox vs. St. Louis Cardinals (A&E Home Video) NR

MLB Superstars Show You Their Game (Sony) NR

Play Ball! The Authentic Little League Baseball Guide — Basic Hitting (Peter Pan) NR

WEB SITES

Pujols Family Foundation
www.pujolsfamilyfoundation.org/
Official site of Albert Pujols

St. Louis Cardinals: The Official Site
www.stlcardinals.com/
The Cards' official Web site

INDEX

About the Author

Geoffrey M. Horn has been a fan of music, movies, and sports for as long as he can remember. He has written more than two dozen books for young people and adults, along with hundreds of articles for encyclopedias and other works. He lives in southwestern Virginia, in the foothills of the Blue Ridge Mountains, with his wife, their collie, and four cats. He dedicates this book to Ed Cornbleet, a loyal friend and devoted Cardinals' fan.